I0410383

June 2014

MILITARY SEXUAL TRAUMA

Improvements Made, but VA Can Do More to Track and Improve the Consistency of Disability Claim Decisions

GAO Highlights

Highlights of GAO-14-477, a report to congressional requesters

MILITARY SEXUAL TRAUMA

Improvements Made, but VA Can Do More to Track and Improve the Consistency of Disability Claim Decisions

Why GAO Did This Study

In 2012, 1 in 5 female and 1 in 100 male veterans told VA that they had experienced sexual abuse in the military. Referred to as military sexual trauma or MST, such abuse can result in disabling conditions like PTSD, which may entitle a veteran to VA benefits. Yet, establishing that MST occurred—a prerequisite for approving these claims—can be difficult, given that servicemembers may be unwilling to file formal complaints. In 2002, VA broadened the scope of allowable evidence for MST-related claims to include indicators, such as behavioral changes. Beginning in 2011, VBA took additional steps to clarify the 2002 changes. GAO was subsequently asked to review these actions.

This report examines: (1) steps VA took to improve MST-related decisions, (2) results of its actions, and (3) the extent it is evaluating the quality of claim decisions. GAO reviewed relevant federal laws, regulations, and guidance; analyzed VA data on MST-related claim decisions (fiscal years 2010-2013); interviewed national VBA and VHA officials, key advocates, and stakeholders, VBA officials at 5 of 57 regional offices (with varying workloads and quality review scores), and VHA examiners associated with 3 of these offices; and reviewed a non-generalizable sample of 18 claim files completed in 2013 for examples of how evidence was evaluated.

What GAO Recommends

GAO is recommending that VA improve training, conduct more outreach, and enhance its MST-related quality reviews and analyses. VA concurred with all of GAO's recommendations.

View GAO-14-477. For more information, contact Daniel Bertoni at (202) 512-7215 or bertonid@gao.gov.

What GAO Found

The Veterans Benefits Administration (VBA), within the Department of Veterans Affairs (VA), has taken several steps to improve decision-making on disability claims involving military sexual trauma (MST) and to rectify past errors. In 2011, VBA began assigning MST-related claims to adjudicators with expertise in complex cases and required them to receive MST-specific training, such as on the broadened scope of evidence allowed since 2002. In 2012, the Veterans Health Administration (VHA) also provided some optional training to medical examiners who provide key input into decisions for such claims. Noting that some MST-related claims may have been erroneously denied prior to the specialization and training of staff, VBA in April 2013 invited 2,667 veterans with denied claims for post-traumatic stress disorder (PTSD) to resubmit them.

According to VBA data, national approval rates for claims based on MST have markedly increased since fiscal year 2010, a change that agency officials attributed to the additional training and a better general understanding of MST requirements. However, GAO found wide variation in approval rates among regional offices, which ranged from 14 to 88 percent in fiscal year 2013. Half of the offices had approval rates close to the average (between 40 and 60 percent), but the rest were higher or lower. While variation does not necessarily signify inconsistency, staff GAO interviewed from four of five offices described ongoing difficulty applying the broadened standards, and GAO found several instances of widely varying interpretations. Both VBA and VHA staff also described variation in the thoroughness of VHA medical exams used by adjudicators to reach decisions. Some VHA medical examiners GAO spoke with required more evidence than others to establish that an MST incident occurred. VBA and VHA staff in almost every office GAO contacted said that further training would be useful, feedback that is consistent with good practices previously identified by GAO and others for reinforcing training. More recently, VHA has decided to make upcoming training on MST-related exams required for all medical examiners who conduct them. With respect to reviewing previously denied claims, VBA was only able to contact veterans whose claims had been denied since September 2010, although those with older claims can also resubmit. VBA's national outreach to other affected veterans was limited to two group meetings with veteran service organizations.

While VBA has taken some steps to evaluate decisions for MST-related claims, its quality reviews and analyses of claim decisions have shortcomings. For example, a 2013 quality review focusing on consistency may under-estimate challenges associated with adjudicating MST claims. Also, due to varying methods and samples, quality reviews conducted to date are insufficient to measure improvement over time—a standard part of internal control. In addition, while VBA analyzes data on national approval rates to gauge the effect of process improvements, GAO's analysis of approval rates by regional office and veteran gender found wide variation. VBA also does not systematically collect data on the number of exams received or why claims are denied—information that could help VBA identify potentially problematic trends. VBA officials said the agency's many competing priorities have precluded additional data collection and analysis to date, but added that they plan to review variations in approval rates in the near future.

_____ United States Government Accountability Office

Contents

Abbreviations

DOD	Department of Defense
MST	military sexual trauma
PTSD	post-traumatic stress disorder
STAR	Systematic Technical Accuracy Review
VA	Department of Veterans Affairs
VBA	Veterans Benefits Administration
VHA	Veterans Health Administration

GAO U.S. GOVERNMENT ACCOUNTABILITY OFFICE

441 G St. N.W.
Washington, DC 20548

June 9, 2014

Congressional Requesters

Trauma resulting from sexual abuse while in military service—referred to as military sexual trauma (MST)—has recently gained attention as a pervasive and continuing problem among U.S. servicemembers. In fiscal year 2012, the Department of Defense (DOD) estimated that about 26,000 servicemembers had experienced some form of unwanted sexual contact, an increase from about 19,000 in fiscal year 2010.[1] At Department of Veterans Affairs (VA) health care facilities in 2012, about 1 in 5 women and 1 in 100 men stated that they experienced sexual abuse in the military.[2] The effects of MST can be severe and long-lasting, and can result in chronic medical conditions such as post-traumatic stress disorder (PTSD), depression, and anxiety disorders. Federal law generally entitles veterans with service-connected disabilities (i.e., injuries or diseases incurred or aggravated in active military service) to disability compensation benefits.[3] This includes disabilities resulting from MST. The Veterans Benefits Administration (VBA), within VA, is charged with processing these claims. From fiscal year 2008 through fiscal year 2013, veterans filed over 29,000 claims for disabilities related to MST. Yet, such claims can be difficult to substantiate, given that servicemembers may be unwilling to file formal complaints at the time of the precipitating incident

---

[1] In the survey DOD used to generate these estimates, the agency defined the term "unwanted sexual contact" as sexual crimes between adults prohibited by military law, ranging from rape to abusive sexual contact. It involves intentional sexual contact that was against a person's will or occurred when the person did not or could not consent. Unlike VA's definition of military sexual trauma (see below), DOD's definition of unwanted sexual contact does not specifically include verbal sexual harassment.

[2] Although rates of MST are higher among women, large numbers of men are also estimated to have experienced sexual abuse.

[3] 38 U.S.C. §§ 1110 and 1131. This does not include disabilities caused by a veteran's own willful misconduct or abuse of alcohol or drugs.

or incidents and, hence, lack official documentation to support their claim.[4]

In response to a court ruling,[5] VA in 2002 revised its regulations for adjudicating PTSD claims related to in-service personal assault, including MST.[6] The revised regulation provides that evidence outside a veteran's service record may be used to corroborate his or her account of MST. As revised, the PTSD regulation acknowledges that VA may take into account, for example, records from civilian law enforcement authorities or rape crisis centers, statements from friends and family members, and evidence of behavioral changes, such as requests for transfer to another military duty assignment.[7]

Even after the 2002 regulatory changes, members of Congress and VBA continued to raise concerns that adjudicators were not accurately and consistently using the broader standard of evidence when adjudicating PTSD claims related to MST. These concerns were substantiated by the agency's own quality assurance reviews, which revealed high error rates for these claims. As a result, VBA in 2011 undertook additional steps to improve decisions for all claims attributed to MST, especially those for PTSD.

You asked us to assess whether VA has adequately addressed concerns about how MST-related claims are adjudicated. This report examines:

---

[4] According to DOD, 2,949 servicemembers filed formal sexual abuse complaints in fiscal year 2012, which represents about 11 percent of the 26,000 servicemembers who were estimated to have experienced unwanted sexual contact during that fiscal year. In fiscal year 2013, DOD reported that 4,113 servicemembers filed formal reports. DOD does not plan to update its estimate of the overall prevalence of unwanted sexual contact until the end of fiscal year 2014.

[5] Patton v. West, 12 Vet. App. 272 (1999).

[6] Post-Traumatic Stress Disorder Claims Based on Personal Assault, 67 Fed. Reg. 10,330 (Mar. 7, 2002). While MST-related claims were an impetus for these regulatory changes, those changes apply to in-service personal assaults generally and not just those that are sexual in nature. They are also specific to PSTD claims and do not impact the standard of evidence for other types of claims related to MST, such as depression or anxiety disorders.

[7] 38 C.F.R. § 3.304(f)(5). The regulation also provides that VA will not deny a PTSD claim based on in-service personal assault without advising the veteran that evidence outside the service record or evidence of behavior changes may be considered and allowing the veteran to furnish it or advise VA of its existence.

1. The steps VA has taken to improve decisions for claims related to military sexual trauma;

2. the results, to date, of VA's actions to improve such decisions; and

3. the extent to which VBA is assessing the quality of its claim decisions related to military sexual trauma.

To identify steps VA has taken to improve MST-related claim decisions, we reviewed related federal laws and regulations as well as guidance, training materials, and planning documents for VBA's improvement initiatives. In addition, we spoke with VBA and Veterans Health Administration (VHA) officials responsible for implementing the initiatives. To examine the results of VA's actions, we analyzed VBA administrative data from fiscal year 2010 to fiscal year 2013 on the number of MST-related claims received, completed, and either approved or denied by disability claimed (e.g., PTSD, depression, or anxiety disorders), gender of the veteran, and VBA regional office.[8] We also spoke with VBA and VHA officials responsible for implementing the improvement initiatives, and with relevant VBA staff in 5 of 57 regional offices to gain their perspective on these initiatives.[9] For the 3 offices that we visited in person, we also conducted telephone interviews with VHA medical examiners affiliated with those VBA offices to learn about exams associated with MST-related claims. In each of those offices, we also reviewed a non-generalizable sample of six claim files completed in 2013 to provide illustrative examples of how VBA adjudicates MST-related claims. We selected claim files from among those recently closed at the time of our site visit and that included approved and denied claims and claims submitted by both men and women. To gain their perspective on

---

[8] These data are collected through VBA's RBA2000 database. When discussing data on MST-related "claims" for the purposes of this report, we are referring to the number of disability claims for medical conditions related to MST filed by veterans. A veteran may have filed multiple cases with the VBA, and these cases may contain multiple claims for physical or mental health conditions related to MST.

[9] We visited the Nashville, Portland, and San Diego VBA regional offices and conducted telephone interviews with Milwaukee and Pittsburgh staff. We selected these offices based on a range of criteria, including performance on VA accuracy and consistency reviews, claims processing time, the number of MST-related claims received, and geographic location, among other things. Staff we spoke with in each office included managers, adjudicators responsible for making MST-related claim decisions, quality review team members who review MST-related claims, and personnel who conduct veteran outreach related to MST.

GAO-14-477 Military Sexual Trauma

VA's handling of MST-related claims, we interviewed representatives from national veteran advocacy organizations, including veteran service organizations, as well as those locally associated with the 3 VBA regional offices we visited.[10] We also weighed VBA's actions against its internal guidance, federal internal control standards, and good practices for implementing training. To assess the extent to which VBA is assessing the quality of its decisions for MST-related claims, we examined VA quality assurance efforts, including results of completed reviews and planning documents for future reviews. We also analyzed VBA administrative data for potential trends in MST-related claim decisions. We assessed the reliability of VBA administrative data used for all our analyses by (1) performing electronic testing for obvious errors in accuracy and completeness, (2) reviewing existing information about the data and the system that produced them, and (3) interviewing agency officials knowledgeable about the data. We determined that the data were sufficiently reliable for the purposes of providing information on trends in claim decisions starting in fiscal year 2010.[11] For additional details on our objectives, scope, and methodology, see Appendix I.

We conducted this performance audit from April 2013 to June 2014 in accordance with generally accepted government auditing standards. Those standards require that we plan and perform the audit to obtain sufficient, appropriate evidence to provide a reasonable basis for our findings and conclusions based on our audit objectives. We believe that the evidence obtained provides a reasonable basis for our findings and conclusions based on our audit objectives.

---

[10] Veteran service organization representatives assist many veterans with filing disability claims. As claimant representatives, veteran service organizations must be accredited by VA and are tasked with providing information on benefits and assistance in applying for them. For more information on VA's accreditation program, see GAO, *VA Benefits: Improvements Needed to Ensure Claimants Receive Appropriate Representation,* GAO-13-643 (Washington, D.C.: Aug. 1, 2013).

[11] Although VBA has collected data on MST-related claims since fiscal year 2008, we used data since fiscal year 2010 because the codes in VBA's data system used to flag MST-related claims were more accurate beginning at that time.

Background

VBA's Disability Compensation Process for MST-Related Claims

While DOD is responsible for prevention, prosecution, and in-service treatment related to sexual abuse, VA is responsible for assisting veterans who experience health problems associated with MST after they leave the military. VA uses the following definition of MST: "psychological trauma, which in the judgment of a mental health professional employed by the Department, resulted from a physical assault of a sexual nature, battery of a sexual nature, or sexual harassment which occurred while the veteran was serving on active duty or active duty for training."[12] Perpetrators may be colleagues, superiors, or individuals not affiliated with the military, and MST can happen during working as well as nonworking hours.

While MST is not, itself, grounds for a disability claim, VA provides compensation for physical or mental health disabilities caused or aggravated by it, such as PTSD or depression.[13] From fiscal year 2010 through fiscal year 2013, PTSD was the most common disability claimed as a result of an incident or incidents of MST, making up about 94 percent of all MST-related claims completed during that time (see fig. 1).

---

[12] 38 U.S.C. § 1720D requires that VA operate a program of counseling and other services for veterans needing them to overcome sexual trauma. VBA has indicated that the definition in this statute should be used for purposes of disability claims. See Department of Veterans Affairs, *Adjudicating Posttraumatic Stress Disorder (PTSD) Claims Based on Military Sexual Trauma (MST),* Training Letter 11-05 (Washington D.C.: June 17, 2013), Attachment. While we use the term "military sexual trauma," which VA uses in some of its guidance, VA regulations generally refer to "in-service personal assault" or "personal assault." 38 C.F.R. § 3.304(f)(5). In addition, the term MST is sometimes used to refer to the precipitating incident or incidents as well as any resulting trauma it causes.

[13] Through VHA, veterans may also receive medical treatment for conditions related to MST.

Figure 1: Disabilities Claimed in Relation to Military Sexual Trauma, Fiscal Year 2010 through Fiscal Year 2013

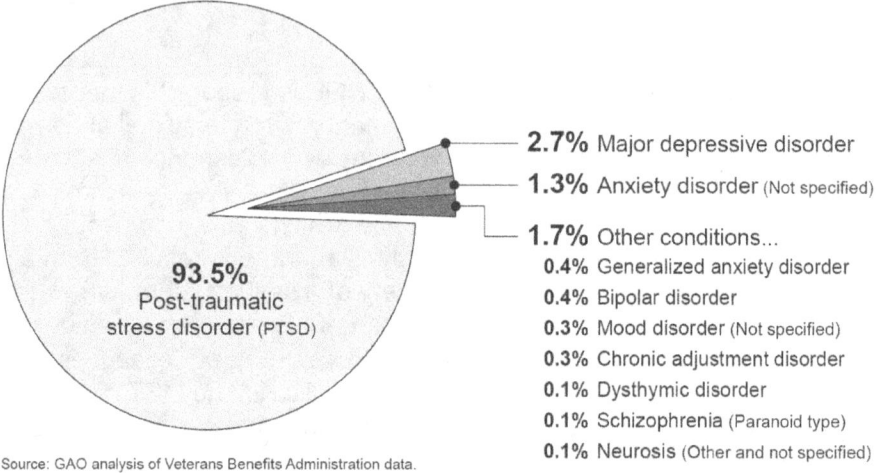

2.7% Major depressive disorder

1.3% Anxiety disorder (Not specified)

1.7% Other conditions...

0.4% Generalized anxiety disorder

0.4% Bipolar disorder

0.3% Mood disorder (Not specified)

0.3% Chronic adjustment disorder

0.1% Dysthymic disorder

0.1% Schizophrenia (Paranoid type)

0.1% Neurosis (Other and not specified)

93.5%
Post-traumatic
stress disorder (PTSD)

Source: GAO analysis of Veterans Benefits Administration data.

As with all disability compensation claims, VBA evaluates MST-related claims through its 57 regional offices. The process starts when a veteran submits a claim and VBA adjudicators help him or her gather relevant evidence.[14] To receive benefits for PTSD related to MST, a veteran must show: (1) a medical diagnosis of PTSD, (2) evidence of an incident or incidents of personal assault while in the military, and (3) a link between current symptoms and the incident or incidents.[15] If sexual assault is documented in the veteran's service record and a recent PTSD diagnosis is present in the veteran's claim file supporting all three of these requirements, VBA adjudicators may approve the claim without extensive research or consultation with medical examiners. However, in most cases related to MST, some or all of this information is not readily available and adjudicators must take additional steps to develop the claim. Specifically, since 2002, VBA's regulations for PTSD claims have expressly allowed for a broad range of evidence to corroborate a veteran's claim that the

---

[14] VBA adjudicators include veterans service representatives who assist veterans during the initial data collection steps in the process and ratings veterans service representatives who work with veterans service representatives to evaluate the evidence and order medical exams, and ultimately decide whether to approve or deny a claim.

[15] 38 C.F.R. § 3.304(f). The regulation refers to an "in-service stressor," and in the MST context, that in-service stressor would be the personal sexual assault.

MST incident or incidents occurred.[16] Adjudicators must consider a range of indicators, whether or not there is anything to support the claim in the veteran's service record.[17] Referred to by the agency as "markers," such indicators include, but are not limited to:

- records from law enforcement authorities, rape crisis centers, mental health counseling centers, hospitals, or physicians;

- pregnancy tests or tests for sexually transmitted diseases;

- statements from family members, roommates, and fellow servicemembers; and

- evidence of behavioral changes, such as requests for transfer to another military duty assignment, deterioration in work performance, and substance abuse.

If the adjudicator does not find any formal reports or markers to suggest that an MST incident occurred, the PTSD claim is denied by the adjudicator without further review because the occurrence of the assault has not been corroborated. Conversely, VA officials stated that adjudicators should order a medical exam if a claim file contains both evidence of the MST incident—such as a marker—and evidence from lay statements or other sources suggesting the veteran has symptoms consistent with a diagnosis of PTSD.

These medical exams are conducted by medical examiners from VBA's sister organization, the Veterans Health Administration (VHA), or by contractors retained by VBA and VHA.[18] Depending on the information needed to decide the claim, the medical examiner is expected to provide the adjudicator with an assessment of one or more of the following: (1) whether the veteran has PTSD; (2) the likelihood that the claimed MST incident occurred (based on his or her interview with the veteran and a review of available markers); and (3) whether there is a link between the diagnosis and the MST incident.

---

[16] VA's regulatory changes do not apply to claims other than PTSD, such as those for depression or anxiety disorders.

[17] 38 C.F.R. § 3.304(f)(5).

[18] A diagnosis of PTSD must be based on criteria contained in the American Psychiatric Association's Diagnostic and Statistical Manual of Mental Disorders, 5th edition.

Using the results of the medical exam and other evidence in the veteran's claim file, the VBA adjudicator determines whether the veteran is entitled to compensation and denies or approves the claim. If the claim is approved, the adjudicator also assigns a percentage rating based on the severity of the claimed disability. If the veteran disagrees with the final claim decision, he or she may submit an appeal.[19] See figure 2 for an overview of the process for adjudicating MST-related claims.

Figure 2: VBA's Disability Compensation Claim Process for PTSD Claims Based on Military Sexual Trauma

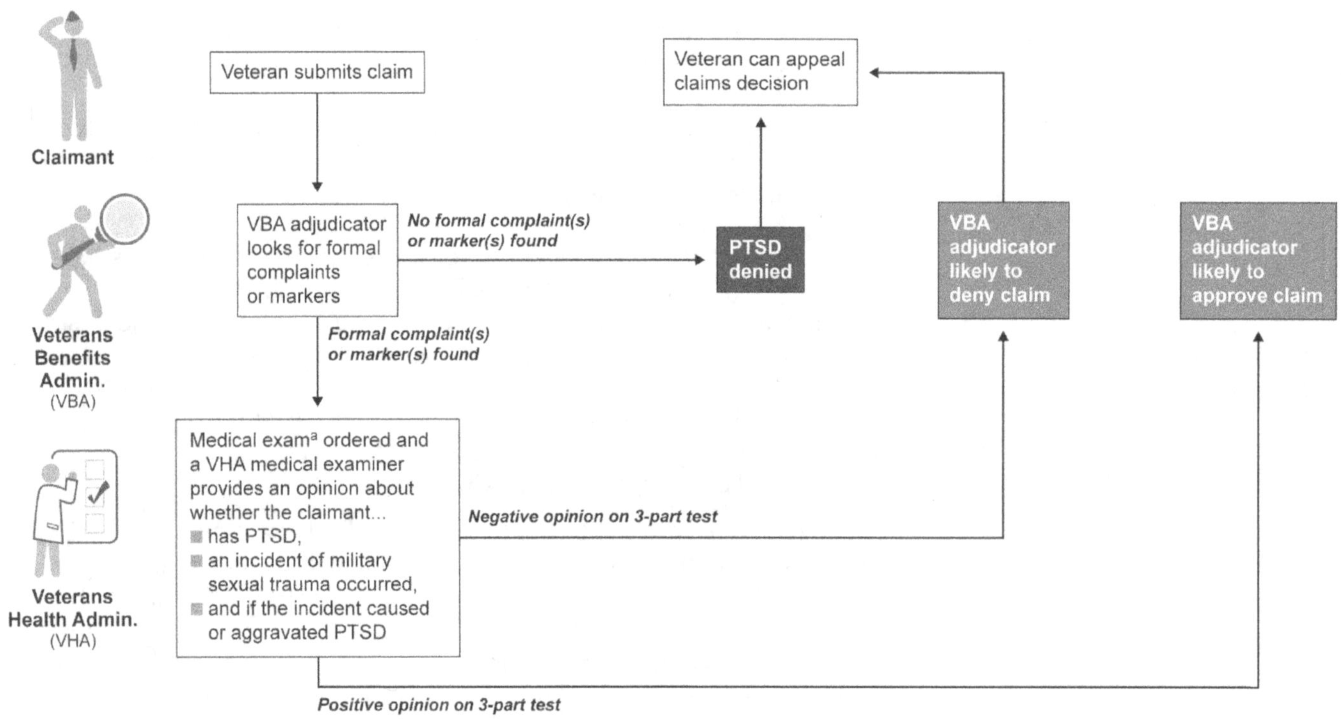

Source: GAO analysis of Department of Veterans Affairs regulations, policies, and guidance.

[a] A medical examiner may not need to assess one or more of these questions if sufficient evidence is present in the file.

[19] A veteran may appeal, in succession, to the Board of Veterans' Appeals, the U.S. Court of Appeals for Veterans Claims, the Court of Appeals for the Federal Circuit, and finally the Supreme Court of the United States. A veteran can also reopen a claim that was denied based on new and material evidence, file a claim for an increase in a service-connected disability, or file a claim for a new disability. A veteran can also file a claim alleging clear and unmistakable error in a prior final regional office or board decision.

VBA's Quality Assurance Programs	VBA has a number of quality assurance programs to help ensure that adjudicators accurately and consistently follow VA regulations and policies. Under the national Systematic Technical Accuracy Review (STAR) program, VBA selects a random sample of all completed claim files each month from each of its regional offices. Using a standard checklist, STAR staff review each claim file and assess whether adjudicators took correct actions during various parts of the process and ultimately made accurate decisions. In addition, in 2012 VBA established local quality review teams in each regional office that assess adjudicator performance using the same review checklist as the national STAR program. For each adjudicator, each month, these reviewers assess five randomly-chosen claims and assess them using a similar process.

Periodically, VBA also conducts targeted reviews to assess adjudicator accuracy or consistency in processing specific types of claims. In August 2011, VBA conducted a special accuracy review in response to concerns that adjudicators were not making accurate decisions for PTSD claims related to MST. The review found errors in 98 of 385 randomly selected claims that had been denied (about 25 percent).[20] In particular, adjudicators should have identified markers and ordered medical exams rather than denied the claim in 61 cases because the files contained markers. The reviewers made several recommendations for improving the adjudication process, such as to: (1) clarify VA policies on markers, (2) build expertise in adjudicating such claims, and (3) develop training.

---

[20] VBA officials described the sample as nationally representative, although they could not provide documentation that would allow us to verify the accuracy of this statement.

GAO-14-477 Military Sexual Trauma

VA Has Taken Several Steps to Improve Processing of Claims Related to MST

VBA Added Specialization and Training for Adjudicators while VHA Provided Some Training to Its Examiners

To help improve adjudicator adherence to processing requirements for MST-related claims, in 2011 VBA began directing regional offices to designate MST specialists from among their adjudicators with experience processing complex claims.[21] The purpose of specialization was to allow regional offices to identify staff with the appropriate skills and sensitivity and afford specialists the opportunity to hone their knowledge of the MST requirements over many claims. At one of the offices we visited, for example, an MST specialist and her backup served as the only points of contact for any communication with MST claimants. These specialists compiled evidence for MST-related claims and then passed the claims on to another MST specialist who identified markers, ordered medical exams, and made final decisions about whether to approve or deny the claims.

Also starting in 2011, VBA developed additional guidance and training for MST specialists (see fig 3). Specifically, in late 2011, the agency issued a guidance letter and rolled out 1.5-hour and 4-hour training sessions on how to process PTSD claims related to MST. VBA also rolled out a one-hour training session on sensitivity in June 2011. All MST specialists were required to take each course once. The guidance letter and trainings on processing claims highlighted the breadth of evidence that may serve as a marker and support that the MST incident occurred. For example, the 4-hour training session described actual cases in which VA's 2011 quality reviewers had found that adjudicators missed markers—such as

---

[21] VBA began to phase in specialization for MST-related claims in 2011, and it was later incorporated into VA's larger claims restructuring initiative. This larger initiative directed regional offices to divide claims and adjudicators into three segmented lanes, based on the type and complexity of the claims. VA considers MST-related claims to be among the most complex, and processes them through the "special operations" lane. The first phase of regional offices implemented the new structure in early 2012, and all regional offices had implemented it by March 2013.

disciplinary problems and childbirth approximately nine months after the alleged MST incident—that should have qualified as markers and triggered a medical exam. The course material for the 1.5-hour session also noted the high degree of judgment required of adjudicators when evaluating whether a claimant's claim file includes markers. Specifically, course materials and presenters stated that there is "no bright line" about what qualifies as a marker and that decisions must be made on a case-by-case basis.

With regard to medical examiners who conduct exams for MST-related claims, VHA has instituted comparatively limited training to date (see fig. 3). The one-hour certification course, required of medical examiners who conduct any type of PTSD exam, devotes 2 of 54 slides to describing how examiners should use markers to assess the likelihood that an MST incident occurred.[22] In collaboration with VBA, VHA had also developed and held a 1.5-hour information session specific to conducting MST-related medical exams. This session was available for on-demand viewing between April 2012 and September 2012. However, because this training is not part of VHA's formal training curriculum, it was optional for in-house medical examiners and not made available to contractors who conduct MST-related exams but are not directly employed by VHA. Over the course of our review, VHA officials said they began developing more formal training on conducting MST-related exams and will start providing it in September 2014. More recently, they also decided to require the training for both in-house examiners and contractors.

---

[22] Medical examiners specialize in conducting exams for certain types of conditions, such as PTSD, but do not further specialize by the type of traumatic event that may have caused the PTSD, such as MST or combat.

Figure 3: Training for VBA Adjudicators and VHA Medical Examiners Regarding Claims Related to Military Sexual Trauma (MST)

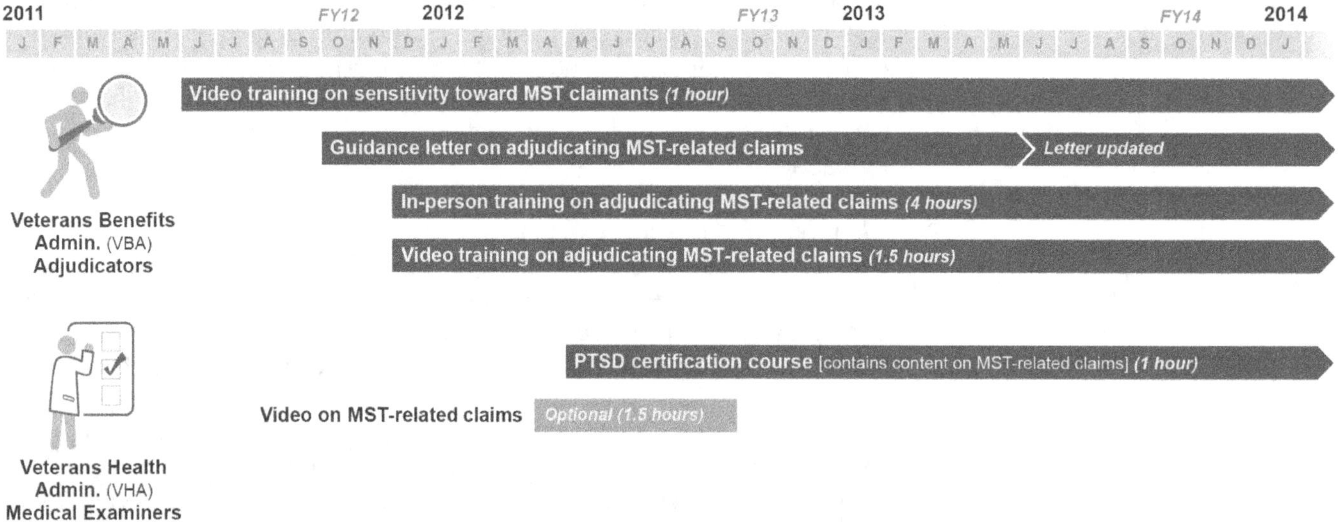

Source: GAO analysis of Department of Veterans Affairs documents and interviews.

VBA Has Notified Some Veterans of the Opportunity to Resubmit Previously Denied Claims

VBA began allowing veterans to resubmit previously denied PTSD claims related to MST in April 2013. While veterans always had the option of resubmitting denied claims to VBA if, for example, they obtained new evidence, this initiative is unique in that it does not require veterans to provide any additional information. The initiative was designed to correct any development errors that had occurred before VBA undertook its specialization and training initiatives. VBA sent 2,667 notification letters to veterans whose PTSD claims related to MST were denied between September 2010 and April 2013. VBA officials also told us they provided the veterans' information to the veteran service organizations that represented them during the original claim process. (For the content of the notification letter, see app. II). While veterans whose claims were denied prior to September 2010 were also eligible to resubmit, VBA officials said most of these veterans did not receive notification letters because the agency did not systematically track such claims as being related to MST.

Since Improvements, Approval Rates Have Increased Nationally yet Vary Widely by Region

Approval Rates for MST-Related Claims Increased Nationwide

Our review of VBA data shows that national approval rates for all types of claims related to MST have increased since fiscal year 2010, almost doubling during that time period. In addition, the approval rates for PTSD claims related to MST have also become more comparable to PTSD claims related to other stressors, such as combat (see fig. 4).[23]

---

[23] VA regulations outline evidentiary requirements for PTSD claims and special evidentiary rules for PTSD claims based on: 1) PTSD diagnosed in-service, 2) combat, 3) fear of hostile military or terrorist activity, 4) status as prisoner of war, and 5) in-service personal assault, which would include MST. 38 C.F.R. § 3.304(f).

Figure 4: Approval Rates for PTSD Claims Related to Military Sexual Trauma versus Other Stressors, Fiscal Year 2010 through Fiscal Year 2013

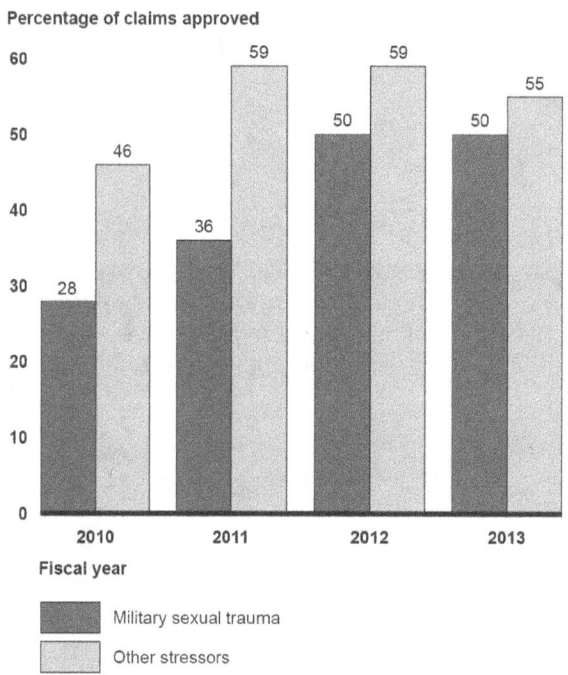

Source: GAO analysis of Veterans Benefits Administration data.

While these trends do not necessarily attest to the accuracy of claim decisions or establish whether any specific initiatives caused the change, VBA officials said they believe the trends indicate that the initiatives are working. Specifically, the new guidance and training on MST-related requirements highlighted the many sources that could be used as markers and lead to medical exams, and officials thought this led to the increased approval rates. They also viewed the increased comparability with other types of PTSD claims as a sign that veterans are having less difficulty establishing that an MST incident occurred than in the past.

Almost all VBA regional office staff we spoke with said that the specialization and training helped reinforce or clarify MST-related requirements. For example, adjudicators in three of five offices we spoke with specifically noted that it was useful to collaborate with other MST specialists about whether evidence qualified as a marker. At the same time, a few regional staff members and veteran service organization representatives expressed concern that MST specialists are being held to the same performance standards for timeliness as other adjudicators and, as such, may prioritize speed over quality. In terms of training and guidance, adjudicators or managers in three of the five offices we spoke with cited the written guidance on MST-related claims as particularly helpful for making decisions about markers and other requirements. We also found that VA followed a number of good practices in developing and implementing its training.[24] For example, the agency developed training content based on its research on errors commonly made with MST-related claims, and the Under Secretary for Benefits publicized the importance of the training.

Approval Rates Varied by Region and Some Adjudicators and Medical Examiners Have Interpreted Processing Requirements Differently

While national approval rates have risen, our analysis of VBA data shows wide variation in approval rates among regional offices. Regional office approval rates for MST-related claims varied from about 14 to 88 percent in fiscal year 2013, and although about half of the offices had approval rates close to the average (between 40 and 60 percent), the rest were higher or lower (see fig. 5).[25]

---

[24] GAO, *Human Capital: A Guide for Assessing Strategic Training and Development Efforts in the Federal Government,* GAO-04-546G (Washington, D.C.: Mar. 1, 2004). GAO developed this guide through consultations with government officials and experts in the private sector, academia, and nonprofit organizations; examinations of laws and regulations related to training and development in the federal government; and reviewing the sizeable body of literature on training and development issues, including previous GAO products on a range of human capital topics.

[25] The results are not specific to PTSD claims, although nationally, 94 percent of MST-related claims are for PTSD. These results reflect all 57 regional offices. When we excluded offices with fewer than 20 MST-related claims, we found that the range of approval rates remained the same.

Figure 5: Range of Regional Office Approval Rates for Claims Related to Military Sexual Trauma in Fiscal Year 2013

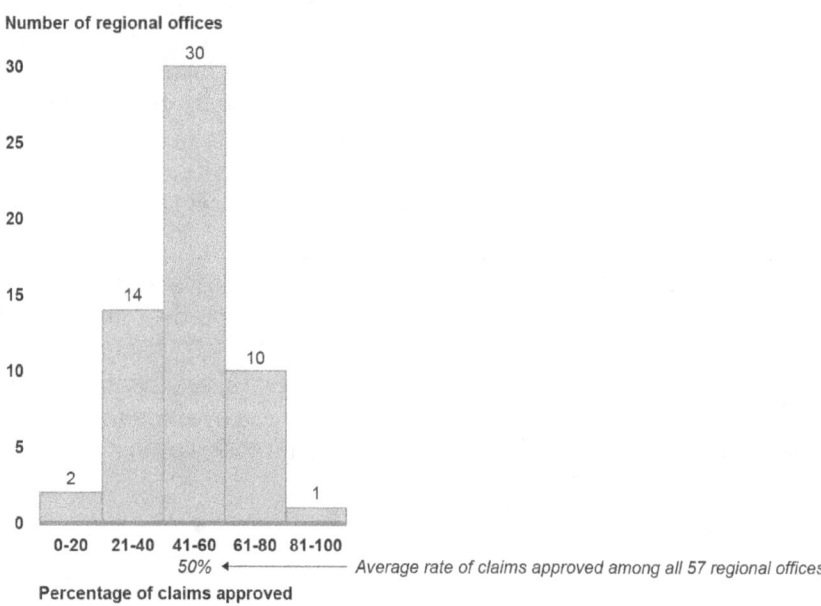

Source: GAO analysis of Veterans Benefits Administration data.

Some variation in approval rates may be expected given that, for example, offices may receive claims with differing characteristics or strengths of evidence. As such, high denial rates or high approval rates do not necessarily equate to inappropriate denials or approvals. However, the extent of the variation raises the question of whether the data reflect real differences in evidence or differences in how the requirements are interpreted and applied. VBA officials we asked said that such variation could result at least in part from inconsistent implementation of MST specialization across regions, varied understanding of how to identify markers, and less experienced adjudicators in some locations.

Our interviews and observations suggest that VBA adjudicators sometimes differ in how they interpret MST-related requirements and make approval decisions. Adjudicators or quality review staff in four of five offices we spoke with said that—even with better guidance and training—identifying markers remains a difficult task. We also learned of cases where adjudicators varied widely in their interpretation of what qualified as a marker, particularly with regard to elapsed time. Specifically:

- An MST adjudicator in one regional office told us she only counts evidence as a marker if it occurred within 2 months of the stated MST incident. However, VBA guidance does not provide a specific time frame for markers.

- In one 2013 claim file we reviewed, the adjudicator had not considered as a marker an HIV test taken 2 months before the veteran claimed that the MST incident occurred. Two supervisors reviewing the file with us said that a different adjudicator may well have considered the test to be a marker, given its proximity to the claimed date and the possibility that the veteran forgot the precise date of the MST incident.

- An MST adjudicator in another regional office told us that she once counted as a marker a pregnancy test that occurred 2 years after the cited MST incident. She said that she had initially determined that the test was not a marker, but received an error report for this from national quality review staff, perhaps because veterans with PTSD may not remember the exact date of the MST incident. She said she disagreed with this error, but reversed her decision. Since that error report, the adjudicator and quality review staff in the regional office said adjudicators' definition of what qualifies as a marker has been very expansive.

- In one of the offices we interviewed, quality review staff said that "vague" complaints of pain or anxiety around the time of the MST incident would, in their view, qualify as markers. However, they described claim files from other offices in which the adjudicator did not consider such complaints to be markers.

- A key VBA official involved in developing agency policy on MST-related claims said that medical records documenting PTSD diagnoses related to MST should be interpreted as markers, even if they occurred many years after the claimed MST incident. However, at least 2 of the 15 claims made in 2013 that we reviewed included medical treatment records of this type that were not treated as markers.

The high degree of judgment required for identifying and weighing markers, as acknowledged in training and by officials with whom we spoke, could account for some variation in decision-making. For example, supervisors in one regional office told us that, hypothetically, two adjudicators could come to opposite conclusions about whether a piece of evidence qualified as a marker, and both decisions might comply with the

VA requirements. Nonetheless, the importance of consistent decision-making has been underscored by VBA's quality assurance plan, our former evaluation of VBA disability claim processing, and the Institute for Defense Analyses.[26] Adjudicators and regional office quality review staff in almost every office we interviewed cited actions that could further clarify their understanding, given the relative complexity of MST-related cases and the grey areas involved in identifying markers. They suggested, for example, refresher courses and the opportunity to see examples of the errors found during quality assurance reviews as a way to reinforce training. This is consistent with Office of Personnel Management guidance and our past work, which state that training and guidance should be reinforced or adjusted in circumstances where staff members remain confused about their responsibilities or when there is a gap between desired and actual practice.[27]

We also heard concerns that VHA medical examiners vary in the thoroughness of their reviews. VBA adjudicators generally rely on examiners' assessments when deciding whether to approve a claim, and staff from four of five offices expressed concern about the quality of some medical examiners' opinions. For example, quality review staff in one office noted that medical examiners vary in how thoroughly they sift through the claim files to identify markers. Seven of the nine medical examiners we spoke with also noted that their colleagues vary in their level of thoroughness in reviewing claims related to MST. For example, one medical examiner cited examples of examiners who complete exams in 15 minutes whereas she said it should take multiple hours, if done correctly. The medical examiner noted that less thorough reviews might lead to less informed assessments.

Moreover, medical examiners we spoke with cited different evidentiary thresholds for providing a positive opinion about the occurrence of the MST incident. Five of the nine medical examiners we spoke with said if they do not find specific evidence of a marker in a veteran's claim file,

---

[26] See GAO, *Veterans' Disability Benefits: VA Has Improved Its Programs for Measuring Accuracy and Consistency, but Challenges Remain,* GAO-10-530T (Washington, D.C,: Mar. 24, 2010) and Institute for Defense Analyses, *Independent Assessment of the Quality Assurance Program in the Department of Veterans Affairs,* IDA Paper P-4744 (Washington, D.C.: July 2011).

[27] Office of Personnel Management, *Training Evaluation Field Guide: Demonstrating the Value of Training at Every Level* (Washington, D.C.: January 2011) and GAO-04-546G.

they will not provide a positive opinion about the occurrence of the MST incident. For example, two of these examiners said that they do not always agree with markers identified by the adjudicator and, in those cases, may spend hours sifting through the files to identify their own markers. If they do not find any markers after this search, they told us they would not provide a positive opinion about the occurrence of the MST incident. Alternatively, three other examiners said that they may still provide a positive opinion that the MST incident occurred if they believe the veteran but cannot find evidence in the file.[28] Given these variations, veterans may have differing chances of getting positive opinions that the MST incident occurred, depending on a given examiner's approach. Almost all of the examiners we spoke with said that more training on identifying markers would be useful. While all examiners conducting PTSD exams receive required training that includes high level information about MST-related exams, VHA's more detailed information session on the topic was optional for VHA medical examiners and not offered to contractors at the time of our review.

Despite variation in examiner training and practices, VBA does not collect information that would help determine the extent to which MST-related claims are handled appropriately or consistently by VHA examiners. For example, VBA does not track the number of exams that adjudicators return to the medical examiner because the examiner's opinion was deemed confusing or incomplete. At the same time, such information might provide a low estimate of less thorough exams because some examiners said that exams are only returned if they have very pronounced errors or omissions.

Veterans May Be Unaware of the Opportunity to Resubmit Previously Denied Claims

Few veterans to whom VBA sent notification letters had resubmitted their previously denied claims as of March 26, 2014 (see fig. 6). According to VBA analysis, 587 of the 2,667 veterans to whom VBA sent notification letters resubmitted their claims between May 1, 2013 and March 26, 2014. VBA made decisions on resubmissions from 429 of these veterans

---

[28] We did not explicitly ask the other two examiners about their threshold for providing a positive opinion about whether the MST incident occurred.

and overturned original denials for 150 of them. Resubmissions from the remaining 158 veterans were pending.[29]

Figure 6: Number of Veterans Sent Notification Letters Regarding Previously Denied PTSD Claims Related to Military Sexual Trauma and Claims Resubmitted and Resolved between May 1, 2013 and March 26, 2014

Source: GAO analysis of Veterans Benefits Administration data.

Some veterans who received notification letters may not resubmit their claims because the letters were confusing or the process was too emotionally taxing to revisit, according to staff from five veteran advocacy organizations and three VBA regional offices. For example, one regional staff member characterized the notification letters as impersonal and expressed concern that they did not provide a direct phone number to VBA staff with experience assisting MST claimants. Staff from another regional office noted that reopening a claim would require the veteran to revisit very painful memories. Given this, veterans may be unwilling to risk having their claim denied a second time.

Furthermore, an undetermined number of eligible veterans did not receive notification letters and may be unaware of the opportunity to resubmit their claims. Veterans with claims denied before September 2010 did not

---

[29] VBA officials said that veterans resubmitting claims may experience some delays because adjudicators are currently prioritizing claims that have been pending for a year or more.

GAO-14-477 Military Sexual Trauma

receive letters because prior to that time, VA data systems did not systematically flag claims as MST-related. Between May 1 and December 2, 2013, VBA made decisions on 174 resubmitted claims from veterans who were not sent notification letters, such as those with claims denied before September 2010. However, it is unclear what proportion of older denied MST-related claims this number represents, given the limitations with VBA's data tracking. It is also unknown whether these claims were resubmitted in response to the initiative or because they were already eligible for resubmission due to new evidence. Moreover, even veterans with newer claims may not have received notification letters if they moved since submitting their original claims to VBA and providing a mailing address.

VBA's national efforts to inform veterans who did not receive notification letters were limited to two meetings with national veteran service organization representatives in June 2013. VBA did not require that regional offices publicize the initiative and we did not see any examples of targeted outreach related to this initiative at the five offices we visited. Local veteran service organization representatives we spoke with said that few to no veterans had approached them about the resubmission initiative. Although these local organizations play a key role in informing veterans about benefits and assisting them with claims, for one VBA regional office, only 1 of the 10 representatives we spoke with had heard about the initiative. At the national level, most veteran service organizations we spoke with also said they knew little about the initiative. An official from one of the organizations said they heard about the initiative by chance and subsequently publicized it on the organization's Facebook page. Keeping stakeholders—such as veterans and veteran service organizations—informed about initiatives is a key component of internal control and important for ensuring that eligible veterans know about available opportunities.[30] Representatives from two veteran advocacy organizations and adjudicators from one regional office we spoke with said that VBA should conduct more outreach regarding this initiative, including posting flyers in VHA medical centers, where veterans—including those with denied MST-related claims—may visit to receive counseling or other services.

---

[30] GAO, *Standards for Internal Control in the Federal Government*, GAO/AIMD-00-21.3.1 (Washington, D.C.: Nov. 1, 1999).

VBA's Evidentiary Requirements Evoke Differing Concerns outside and within the Agency

In our interviews outside and within VBA, we found continuing, albeit differing, concerns about the fairness of the evidentiary requirements for MST-related claims. First, stakeholders outside and within the agency disagreed on whether the requirements for PTSD claims attributed to MST were too stringent, particularly when compared to those for PTSD claims attributed to other stressors. On the other hand, staff within VBA expressed concern that MST-related evidentiary requirements for mental health disabilities other than PTSD were more stringent than those for PTSD because markers cannot be used for other mental health disabilities.

Concerns Regarding the Evidentiary Requirements for PTSD Claims

Stakeholders we interviewed expressed divergent views about the fairness of the requirements for PTSD claims related to MST and the implications for expanding them. Outside of the agency, representatives from four of five veteran advocacy organizations we interviewed expressed concern that the requirement to substantiate an MST incident is still difficult to meet for many with valid claims.[31] Some of these representatives said that even markers can be difficult to find or may not exist, since veterans may have initially tried to hide their experience due to fear of reprisal or feelings of shame or embarrassment, among other reasons. These representatives contrasted the requirements for other PTSD claims with those for PTSD claims related to MST. For example, they noted that for PTSD claims related to fear of hostile military or terrorist activity, a veteran's own testimony alone generally may establish the claimed incident (i.e., in-service stressor),[32] and took the position that this constitutes a far lower burden of proof than for PTSD claims related to MST. However, in contrast to these perspectives, VBA officials pointed out that in such cases, a veteran's own testimony alone may establish the claimed in-service stressor only if that stressor is consistent with the places, types, and circumstances of the veteran's service. For example, officials said that the veteran's testimony could be sufficient if the military record established that the veteran was located in an area where the claimed stressful military event could have occurred (see fig. 7). VBA officials noted that the 2002 allowance for MST markers was the agency's way of broadening the range of permissible evidence while still requiring

---

[31] The fifth organization did not have a position on this issue.

[32] 38 C.F.R. § 3.304(f)(3).

some level of proof beyond the veteran's own testimony. They said that to eliminate or further ease these requirements would eliminate the agency's ability to verify the claim, as is required for all other types of claims.[33]

Figure 7: Examples of Credible Supporting Evidence Needed to Substantiate that an In-Service Stressor Occurred by Type of PTSD Claim[a]

Type of PTSD claim	Military records	Testimonial	Other corroborating	Medical examiner confirmation	Outcome
Combat	Veteran treated for combat-related wounds, or earned medals or awards	Veteran's description of what happened in combat			*Claim likely approved*
Fear of hostile activity Military or terrorist	Information on veteran's duty station and/or squad activities	Veteran's description of what happened on duty		Positive opinion that stressful event likely occurred	*Claim likely approved*
Personal assault Including military sexual trauma (MST)	Formal complaint of sexual assault made by veteran		"Markers"	Positive opinion that MST likely occurred[b]	*Claim likely approved*

Source: GAO analysis of Department of Veterans Affairs regulations, policies, and procedures.

[a] To receive benefits for all types of PTSD claims, a veteran must also show a diagnosis of PTSD and a causal association between the diagnosis and the stressful event.

[b] Such an exam would include interviewing the veteran about the MST incident.

Concerns Regarding the Evidentiary Requirements for Other Mental Health Claims

VBA staff we interviewed in all five regional offices expressed concern that the MST-related evidentiary requirements for mental health disabilities other than PTSD are more stringent than those for PTSD. Because VA's 2002 regulatory changes allowing for markers only apply to

---

[33] Legislation pending in Congress would address the evidentiary requirements for PTSD claims related to MST. On June 4, 2013, the House of Representatives passed H.R. 671, the Ruth Moore Act of 2013, which includes a statement of the sense of the Congress that the VA should update and improve its regulations related to MST. In the Senate, S. 294, also entitled the Ruth Moore Act of 2013, would amend current law to provide, for example, that under certain conditions a veteran's lay testimony alone may establish the occurrence of MST. S. 294 was introduced and referred to the Committee on Veterans' Affairs on February 13, 2013.

PTSD claims, staff said that MST-related claims for other mental health disabilities, such as depression or anxiety disorders, are more difficult to substantiate. They explained that, unlike PTSD, a claimant diagnosed with depression or an anxiety disorder must have evidence other than markers to connect his or her disability to military service, such as medical records related to treatment received while the veteran was in the military. For example, if a veteran has no in-service treatment history, is diagnosed with depression years after leaving service, and says that the depression is a result of MST, he or she would need to have documentation such as a formal complaint of sexual assault in his or her military records to substantiate that the event occurred in military service and evidence linking the assault to the depression. In one file we reviewed, a veteran's PTSD claim related to MST was denied when the medical examiner diagnosed the veteran with depression instead of PTSD. The letter sent to the veteran regarding the decision noted that the markers would have served as evidence to support the occurrence of MST if the diagnosis had been PTSD. However, the letter said the markers could not be used because the veteran was subsequently diagnosed by the medical examiner with depression. No formal complaint of sexual assault was present in the file. Regional staff in four offices expressed concern that it is difficult for them to substantiate claims for other mental health disabilities that are related to MST, given that veterans infrequently file formal complaints of sexual assault while in service.[34]

VBA plans to reevaluate its evidentiary requirements for non-PTSD mental health claims related to MST, according to officials. They said the 2002 regulatory changes allowing for MST markers were aligned with broader evidentiary requirements for all PTSD claims—which include other types of in-service events, such as combat, and are also specific to PTSD—and the agency did not intentionally exclude other types of mental health claims. One official noted that any changes would involve reviewing relevant diagnostic criteria and considering any implications for mental health claims that are unrelated to MST.

---

[34] While our analysis of VBA data suggests similar approval rates for PTSD and non-PTSD mental health claims attributed to MST, VBA data do not allow for comparisons of approval rates by whether non-PTSD mental health conditions were diagnosed in or post-service.

VBA Has Not Optimized Opportunities to Evaluate or Collect Information about MST-Related Decisions

VBA Has Conducted Few Quality Reviews of MST-Related Claims

Since conducting the 2011 quality review that triggered its improvement initiatives, VBA has conducted two more quality reviews of MST-related claims, but both have limitations. VBA conducted the first of these reviews in October 2012, which examined whether adjudicators took appropriate actions with respect to claims that received a medical exam and were subsequently denied. While it provided some information on errors made by adjudicators, for example, in interpreting medical examiner opinions, it did not provide any information about the quality of the adjudication process for approved claims or claims that were denied without a medical exam. However, adjudicators in at least one of the regional offices we visited raised concerns about the potential for inappropriate approvals, in addition to inappropriate denials. VBA officials said this review of denied claims was conducted at the request of Congress, which was particularly interested in claims denied following a medical exam.

VBA conducted its second review in December 2013, which assessed the consistency of adjudicators' knowledge of how to process MST-related claims. Adjudicators present on the day the review was administered were given a case scenario involving a PTSD claim related to MST and a related questionnaire that probed errors found in prior reviews. They were asked to identify relevant markers from a multiple-choice list, and to determine whether a medical exam should be ordered and whether the case should be approved, denied, or deferred for additional information. VBA found that 85 percent of 755 adjudicators correctly approved the case, 14 percent incorrectly deferred their decision to approve or deny the claim, and 1 percent incorrectly denied it.[35] VBA is requiring that all adjudicators who provided incorrect answers to the questionnaires receive more training by the end of April 2014. While this review provided some information on common errors made by adjudicators, the results may underestimate the challenge of adjudicating MST-related claims, given that responding to multiple choice questions about a hypothetical case may be less difficult than sifting through a real claim file to identify markers, order an exam, and make a decision. In addition, because the review was administered as a one-time test and was not mandatory, the results may not include adjudicators who were absent on the day of the review or did not participate for other reasons.

In addition to these limitations, VBA's reviews of MST-related claims have not allowed it to monitor the quality of its processes over time, a standard part of internal control and best practice for ensuring that associated training is relevant and sufficient.[36] The results of the MST-specific quality reviews discussed above are not comparable because they measured quality in different ways. Similarly, neither can be compared with the 2011 quality review completed prior to VA's improvement initiatives because (1) the quality reviews of denied claims were selected from overlapping time periods and (2) the consistency study used a different measure of quality.[37] Furthermore, while VBA does conduct longitudinal reviews of the accuracy and consistency of all claim files through its national STAR and local quality reviews,[38] only a limited number of MST-related claims are reviewed each month, if at all, and VBA does not specifically track the inclusion or results of MST-related claims within these reviews.

---

[35] The review included one questionnaire for adjudicators who gather evidence (veterans service representatives and related quality review staff) and one questionnaire for adjudicators who determine whether to approve the claim (ratings veterans service representatives and related quality review staff.) The 755 adjudicators who answered the question were from 53 of 57 regional offices.

[36] GAO/AIMD-00-21.3.1 and Office of Personnel Management, *Training Evaluation Field Guide: Demonstrating the Value of Training at Every Level.*

[37] Specifically, the 2011 and 2012 reviews of denied claims both focused on different types of denied claims—all denied claims versus those that were denied after receiving an exam—that were completed between 2008 and the time that each review was conducted, and thus cannot show change in quality over time.

[38] Results from national STAR and local quality reviews are used to track performance trends within and/or among all regional offices.

At the time of our review, VBA officials were planning to conduct two additional reviews of MST-related claims to identify training needs. Specifically, after calculating regional office approval rates at our request, VBA officials decided to assess the quality of claim decisions among offices with relatively high or rising denial rates. The agency planned to review approximately 500 claims from 20 offices, starting in April 2014. Further, officials said VBA will conduct an additional quality review in September or October 2014. They said this review will focus on randomly selected PTSD claims related to MST and include both those approved and denied. However, as with past reviews, these planned reviews will focus on different subsets of claims, and therefore, it is unclear how the agency will use them to monitor trends over time.

VBA Has Studied Its Approval Rates for PTSD Claims Nationally, but Has Not Analyzed Available Data by Regional Office or Veteran Gender

In response to congressional requests, VBA has examined trends in approval rates for PTSD claims related to MST as well as those related to combat and other stressors. Both VBA's and our analyses show that approval rates for PTSD claims related to MST have increased, and are becoming more comparable to those for other types of PTSD claims. VBA officials said the increased approval rates show the effects of VBA's specialization and training initiatives.

Nevertheless, VBA has not analyzed other available data that could help it identify potential problem areas to target training needs, such as approval rates by regional office and veteran gender for all MST-related claims. As noted earlier, our analysis of existing VBA data found wide variances in approval rates across regional offices, ranging from 14 to 88 percent. In addition, we found that approval rates for MST-related claims from female veterans remained consistently higher than those from males between fiscal years 2010 and 2013 (see fig. 8).[39]

---

[39] Between fiscal years 2010 and 2013, about 63 percent of MST-related claims completed were filed by females, 36 percent were filed by males, and 1 percent was filed by veterans who did not specify their gender.

Figure 8: Percentage of Claims Related to Military Sexual Trauma Approved for Males versus Females, Fiscal Year 2010 through Fiscal Year 2013

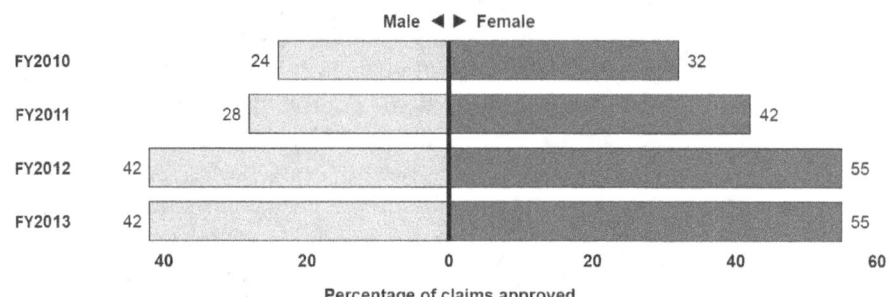

Male ◄ ► Female

	Male	Female
FY2010	24	32
FY2011	28	42
FY2012	42	55
FY2013	42	55

40   20   0   20   40   60

Percentage of claims approved

Source: GAO analysis of Veterans Benefits Administration data.

As discussed earlier, variations in approval rates do not necessarily mean that decisions were inaccurate, as they could be attributed to actual differences among claims and their levels of evidence. However, they do pose reasonable questions as to the level of consistency among adjudicators. VBA officials said the agency's many competing priorities have precluded their following up with more data collection and analysis to date, although they do plan to review variations in approval rates in the near future.

Finally, VBA does not electronically collect information about the number of MST-related claimants who receive medical exams, how often such exams are considered insufficient, and why claims are denied.[40] As noted above, we found instances where VBA adjudicators may vary in how they interpret requirements for identifying markers and ordering an exam, and where VHA medical examiners may vary in how they conduct such exams. Without systematically collecting information about exams and why claims were ultimately denied, VBA cannot identify national or

---

[40] VBA does collect some high-level data on reasons for claim denials, but VBA officials said it provides very limited information on actual reasons for each claim. Current codes to capture reasons for denials in VBA's data system include, for example, "not in the line of duty," "not aggravated by service," "no diagnosis," and "not incurred/caused by service."

regional trends in these areas. Officials acknowledged that MST has become a more prominent topic in recent years, particularly within Congress, and that VBA will collect and analyze more data as needed.[41]

Conclusions

In adjudicating claims related to sexual assault, VA faces the difficult task of assessing events for which there is often no concrete evidence. The difficulty of the task reveals the pernicious nature of MST: servicemembers may fear the repercussions of reporting an experience that was, itself, traumatic. This fear can be confounded if the perpetrator was a colleague or someone in a position of power, and this betrayal of trust can inflict profound confusion and pain.

VA has taken a number of important steps to redress the dearth of evidence in a veteran's service record, both going forward with adjudicating new claims and acknowledging the potential for error in prior MST-related claim decisions. However, its decision to broaden the scope of allowable evidence—and thereby reduce inappropriate denials—brings its own challenges. Evaluating such a range of evidence requires expertise and a substantial degree of judgment by adjudicators and examiners, and some variation in determinations may be expected by virtue of the different circumstances surrounding each case. However, a level of inconsistency may occur that is not acceptable, especially if a veteran's chance of getting a claim approved is contingent on the particular adjudicator or medical examiner responsible for the review. Yet, to completely avoid such inconsistencies could require either a highly prescriptive set of rules for weighing the available evidence of sexual abuse, or, conversely, removing altogether the requirement for evidence of the assault—actions that carry their own risks and would require careful decision making.

Even without sweeping changes to policy, there is substantial opportunity to make process changes that could better ensure benefits are appropriately awarded to veterans with valid MST-related claims. In contrast to VA's actions to date, which largely have been taken in response to external requests, a more proactive and systematic approach could further dispel confusion among adjudicators and examiners, identify errors, and inform veterans of opportunities to resubmit denied claims.

---

[41] Both House and Senate versions of pending legislation, the Ruth Moore Act of 2013 (H.R. 671 and S. 294), would require VA to report data on MST-related claims as well as information on employee training related to MST.

Specifically, without more thorough and continuous training, some adjudicators and medical examiners are likely to remain confused about what qualifies as evidence. In addition, designing quality reviews to track trends over time, more fully analyzing data on MST-related claim decisions, and exploring options for collecting additional data could help VA flag potential areas of inconsistency for more careful review. Meanwhile, the limited outreach to veterans denied benefits for an MST-related claim could leave many unaware of new opportunities to have their claims reassessed under the broadened evidentiary requirements.

Recommendations for Executive Action

The Acting Secretary of Veterans Affairs should direct the Under Secretary for Benefits to

- expand existing training and guidance to adjudicators responsible for MST-related claims by, for example, providing mandatory refresher courses or regularly distributing examples of relevant errors identified from quality assurance reviews.

- develop a plan for conducting more comprehensive quality reviews of MST-related claims that allows the agency to identify problem areas, target improvement efforts, and track performance over time.

- further analyze existing data on MST-related claim decisions by, for example, determining approval rates by regional office and veteran gender.

- explore ways to systematically collect additional data on MST-related claims that might allow the agency to better track consistency. Such data could include reasons for denials, whether claim evaluations included a medical exam, and how often related medical exam reports are returned to VHA for clarification or deemed insufficient.

- expand outreach to veterans who are eligible to resubmit their previously denied PTSD claims related to MST. The agency should conduct this outreach in partnership with the Veterans Health Administration or external organizations, such as veteran service organizations.

The Acting Secretary of Veterans Affairs should further direct the Under Secretary for Health to ensure that planned training on conducting MST-related exams is provided to all medical examiners who perform them, including contractors.

Agency Comments and Our Evaluation

We provided a draft of this report to VA for review and comment, and its written comments are reproduced as appendix III in this report. VA generally agreed with our conclusions and concurred with all of our recommendations. The agency outlined how it plans to address our recommendations as follows:

- Regarding our recommendation to expand existing training and guidance to adjudicators, VA said that VBA is in the process of developing refresher training and anticipated that it will be available to staff by August 15, 2014. As VBA finalizes this training, it should consider making the training mandatory to all staff processing MST-related claims or to those whose claim decisions have been found to be in error.

- Regarding our recommendation to develop a plan for conducting more comprehensive quality reviews, VA said that VBA plans to conduct special MST-related reviews twice each year and systematically analyze the results of each review within 4 months of completion. VA said that its current plans were sufficient to implement the recommendation. However, we would need additional information about the planned reviews—such as whether they will employ comparable methodologies and samples of claim files to allow VBA to track performance over time—before considering this recommendation implemented.

- Regarding our recommendation to further analyze existing data on MST-related claim decisions, VA said VBA will review and analyze such data by October 2014 and conduct follow-up analyses every 6 months thereafter.

- Regarding our recommendation to explore ways to systematically collect additional data on MST-related claims, VA said VBA has begun developing such an approach, particularly in terms of tracking reasons why claims are denied. VBA plans to conduct its first analysis in October 2014 with follow-up analyses every 6 months thereafter. VBA and VHA plan to use the information to identify areas where variations in approval rates may result from different interpretations of how to adjudicate claims or conduct medical exams.

- Regarding our recommendation to expand outreach to veterans about the option to resubmit previously denied claims, VA said

VBA will conduct additional outreach by September 30, 2014, working closely with VHA, veteran service organizations, and others.

- Regarding our recommendation that planned training on conducting MST-related exams be provided to all relevant medical examiners, VA outlined plans for ensuring that examiners participate in the training. Specifically, by April 30, 2015, all VHA medical examiners and contractors will be required to take the training and VA medical centers and vendors who employ contractors will be required to certify that examiners completed the training.

VA also provided technical comments, which we incorporated into our report as appropriate.

We are sending copies of this report to the appropriate congressional committees and the Acting Secretary of Veterans Affairs. In addition, the report is available at no charge on the GAO website at http://www.gao.gov.

If you or your staff have any questions about this report, please contact me at (202) 512-7215 or bertonid@gao.gov. Contact points for our Offices of Congressional Relations and Public Affairs may be found on the last page of this report. GAO staff who made key contributions to this report are listed in appendix IV.

Daniel Bertoni
Director, Education, Workforce, and Income Security Issues

List of Requesters

The Honorable Patty Murray
Chairman
Committee on the Budget
United States Senate

The Honorable Bernard Sanders
Chairman
Committee on Veterans' Affairs
United States Senate

The Honorable Jon Runyan
Chairman
Subcommittee on Disability Assistance and Memorial Affairs
Committee on Veterans' Affairs
House of Representatives

The Honorable Mark Begich
United States Senate

The Honorable Richard Blumenthal
United States Senate

The Honorable Jon Tester
United States Senate

The Honorable Chellie Pingree
House of Representatives

Appendix I: Objectives, Scope, and Methodology

The objectives of this report were to examine (1) the steps the Department of Veterans Affairs (VA) has taken to improve decisions for claims related to military sexual trauma (MST), (2) the results, to date, of VA's actions to improve such decisions, and (3) the extent to which the Veterans Benefits Administration (VBA) within VA is assessing the quality of its claim decisions related to MST. To address these objectives, we reviewed related federal laws and regulations as well as guidance, training materials, and planning documents for VA's improvement initiatives. We also reviewed GAO criteria on internal controls, program management, and good practices for implementing training. Further, for all three objectives, we interviewed VBA and Veterans Health Administration (VHA) officials, VBA and VHA regional staff, and national and local advocates. (See below for more information about our interviews). We also reviewed a small sample of completed claim files to obtain examples of the evidence available for establishing the occurrence of MST incidents and VBA and VHA processes to evaluate such evidence. (See below for more information about this claim file review.) To examine the results of the initiatives to date and the extent to which VBA is assessing the quality of claim decisions, we analyzed VBA administrative data on MST-related claim approval rates and spoke with relevant VBA staff. (See below for more information about our review of these data and our efforts to ensure their reliability.) We also reviewed VBA reports about their quality assurance reviews and the resubmission initiative for previously denied claimants. We assessed the reliability of these reports by reviewing related documentation and interviewing agency officials knowledgeable about how they were produced. We determined that the results presented in this report were sufficiently reliable for our purposes.

Interviews

To obtain information relevant to all three objectives, we interviewed VBA officials responsible for developing and disseminating policy, training, and guidance on MST-related claims and quality assurance staff including officials responsible for the Systematic Technical Accuracy Review (STAR) and Quality Review and Consistency Programs. We also spoke with VHA officials responsible for overseeing medical examiners who conduct exams related to VBA disability claim decisions and VHA staff and officials responsible for developing and disseminating medical examiner training on MST-related exams.

In addition, we interviewed managers and staff at the regional level to better understand how MST-related policies and initiatives were implemented. We selected 5 of VBA's 57 regional offices for review. The

offices were selected to reflect a variety of characteristics related to (1)
performance on VA accuracy and consistency reviews,[1] (2) efficiency of
claim processing,[2] (3) number of MST-related claims received,[3] (4) time
elapsed since certain VA initiatives were adopted,[4] and (5) geographical
region.[5] We visited 3 of the selected offices in person (Nashville,
Portland, and San Diego) and conducted interviews with the remaining 2
over the phone (Milwaukee and Pittsburgh). The information obtained
during these interviews is not generalizable to all VBA regional offices.

For all 5 regional offices, we spoke with managers, adjudicators who
specialize in MST-related claims, quality review team members who
review MST-related claims, and personnel who conduct veteran outreach
related to MST. For the 3 offices that we visited in person, we interviewed
one or more VHA psychologists who conduct medical exams for MST-
related claims or provide clarification to VBA adjudicators regarding MST-
related exams completed by others. We also spoke with local veteran
service organization representatives in each of these 3 offices who had
previously worked on MST-related claims.

Outside of VA, we spoke with representatives from national veteran
service organizations and other advocacy groups. These included
representatives from the Disabled American Veterans, Iraq and
Afghanistan Veterans of America, National Veterans Legal Services

---

[1] We used data from VBA's ASPIRE Dashboard to rank regional office performance on
VA's national accuracy and consistency reviews of disability and compensation claim
decisions for May 2013, the most recent data at the time of our selection.

[2] We used data from VBA's ASPIRE Dashboard to rank regional office performance on
the efficiency of claim processing in May 2013. Regional offices were ranked based on the
percentage of backlogged claims, average days of processing time for claims, and
average days pending for claims.

[3] We used data requested from VBA's Office of Field Operations to rank regional offices
on the number of MST-related claims received in fiscal year 2012, the most recent data at
the time of our selection. For this criterion, we focused on selecting regional offices with a
higher number of MST-related claims received, since these types of claims are the focus
of our study.

[4] We used data requested from the Office of Field Operations to rank regional offices
based on the date of adoption of the special operations lanes initiative, which uses
specialized staff to adjudicate MST-related claims.

[5] We used VBA's regional office structure, which categorizes regional offices into eastern,
western, southern, and central regions.

Program, Service Women's' Action Network, and Veterans of Foreign
Wars. We selected interviewees based on the size of the organization
and recommendations from other stakeholders.

Claim File Review

For each of the 3 VBA regional offices we visited in person, we reviewed
a non-generalizable sample of 6 claim files that were completed in 2013
(18 total) to provide illustrative examples of how VBA adjudicates MST-
related claims. These claim files included the evidence collected by
adjudicators, correspondence with the veteran on the status of their claim,
and the decision made on the claim. We selected claim files from among
those recently completed at the time of our visit to each regional office.
We chose files that provided variation in terms of the claimed disability,
decision made on the claim (approval or denial), and veteran gender. Our
sample also included two PTSD claims related to other stressors for
comparison purposes. For each claim file, we documented the disability,
evidence provided to support the claim, key findings from the medical
exam, nature and frequency of correspondence with the veteran, and
decision on whether to approve or deny the claim.

Analysis of VBA Data on Claim Decisions

We obtained and analyzed data from VBA's RBA2000 database for the
following types of disability claim decisions:

- MST-related claims. We obtained data on the number of all MST-
  related claims that were received, completed, and approved or denied
  for each fiscal year from 2008—the earliest year for which VBA has
  data—through 2013. We also obtained breakouts for these data by
  disability claimed, veteran gender, and regional office.

- PTSD claims related to other non-MST stressors. Similar to the data
  for MST-related claims, we obtained data on the number PTSD claims
  related to other stressors that were received, completed, and
  approved or denied for each fiscal year from 2008 through 2013 for
  comparison purposes. We also obtained breakouts for these data by
  veteran gender and regional office.

In requesting data from VBA, we chose to exclude data on decisions
made regarding re-evaluation requests for a higher disability rating
percentage because such decisions are based largely on the diagnoses,
not on whether the claim is MST-related. We chose to report approval
rates by MST-related disability or "claim" rather than unique case or
unique veteran. Each unique case can include claims for multiple

disabilities, and each unique veteran may have multiple cases with claims for multiple disabilities. Therefore, we determined that analysis at the level of individual disabilities provided the most accurate and nuanced information about MST-related decision making.

We assessed the reliability of the data obtained by (1) performing electronic testing for obvious errors in accuracy and completeness, (2) reviewing existing information about the data and the system that produced them, and (3) interviewing agency officials knowledgeable about the data. We determined that the data were sufficiently reliable for purposes of providing information on trends in claim decisions. However, there were several limitations to the data obtained:

- The data obtained may under-represent the number of MST-related claims completed because VBA does not have procedures in place to verify whether adjudicators appropriately flag MST-related claims in the system.

- We chose to report on claim decisions made since fiscal year 2010 due to data reliability concerns about older decisions. Although VBA databases have allowed the agency to track MST-related claims since fiscal year 2008, its tracking system became more accurate in fiscal year 2010. Prior to that time, the codes used to identify MST-related claims only referred to PTSD, and officials expressed concern that adjudicators applied the codes inconsistently. In fiscal year 2010, VBA developed more detailed codes for identifying MST-related claims, including codes that identified claims for both PTSD and other disabilities. The agency also provided more guidance to adjudicators about appropriately applying the codes.

We analyzed VBA data to determine the most common disabilities associated with MST-related claims and examined trends in approval rates. We calculated approval rates by dividing the number of claims approved by the number completed for each type of claim. We examined trends in approval rates nationally as well as by veteran gender and regional office. We chose to include all 57 regional offices in our analyses. To assess whether any individual decision could unduly impact the approval rates in offices with fewer claims, we also conducted an analysis that excluded offices with 20 or fewer claims in fiscal year 2013. We ultimately decided to include the results from these offices after determining that both analyses resulted in the same range of approval rates.

We were unable to determine the causes for variation among regional office rates due to the absence of data on factors that could impact claim decisions—such as the reasons for denial—and the limited number of MST-related claims in each regional office. Trends in approval rates do not necessarily attest to the accuracy of claim decisions, and could be attributed to actual differences among claims and their levels of evidence.

Our analyses focused on completed claims by fiscal year. Since claims may take awhile to complete, sometimes more than a year, in any given year, a large number of cases may be pending and therefore not captured in our analyses for one or more years. Given limitations with the administrative data, we could not analyze whether completed claims differed significantly from pending claims and whether including pending claims would alter the results of our analysis of potential trends in MST-related claim decisions. Figure 9 provides the number of MST-related claims completed, received, and pending in each fiscal year from 2010 through 2013. Information on pending claims was obtained from VBA's MAP-D database, which tracks information on claims still in process. VBA officials said the number of pending MST-related claims may be under-represented. They explained that an adjudicator may not know a claim is related to MST until later on in the process and thus, would not flag it as an MST-related claim in MAP-D.[6]

---

[6] They stated that adjudicators are more likely to have accurate information about a claim's relationship to MST by the time the claim is completed and documented in the RBA2000 database.

**Figure 9: The Number of Claims Related to Military Sexual Trauma Completed,
Received, and Pending, Fiscal Year 2010 through Fiscal Year 2013**

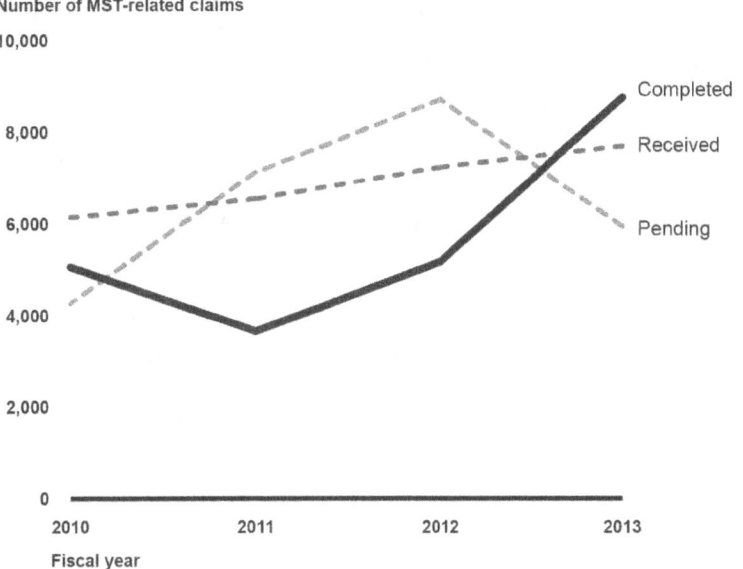

Source: GAO analysis of Veterans Benefits Administration data.

GAO-14-477 Military Sexual Trauma

Appendix II: Text of Notification Letter Sent to Previously Denied Claimants

Veteran XXX,

The Department of Veterans Affairs (VA) records show that you previously filed a disability claim for posttraumatic stress disorder (PTSD) and stated that the stressor was related to sexual trauma experienced in the military.

Although your claim was denied, in VA's continued efforts to assist Veterans, claims for PTSD based on military sexual trauma (MST) are being reviewed. A new review will determine if any evidence was overlooked. Participation in a VA examination may be required.

Please contact your local VA regional office if you would like your PTSD claim reviewed to determine entitlement to service connection.

For convenience, submit the enclosed VA Form 21-4138 (Statement in Support of Claim) and indicate that you would like to have your PTSD claim based on MST reviewed.

If you have any additional evidence to support your claim, including statements from family members or fellow service members, please advise the regional office.

Sincerely,

Thomas J. Murphy
Director, Compensation Service

Appendix III: Comments from the Department of Veterans Affairs

Department of Veterans Affairs
Office of the Secretary

May 15, 2014

Mr. Daniel Bertoni
Director, Education, Workforce, and
 Income Security Issues
U.S. Government Accountability Office
441 G Street, NW
Washington, DC 20548

Dear Mr. Bertoni:

The Department of Veterans Affairs (VA) has reviewed the Government Accountability Office's (GAO) draft report, **"MILITARY SEXUAL TRAUMA: Improvements Made, but VA Can Do More to Track and Improve the Consistency of Disability Claim Decisions"** (GAO-14-477). VA generally agrees with GAO's conclusions and concurs with GAO's recommendations to the Department.

The enclosure specifically addresses GAO's recommendations and provides technical comments to the draft report. VA appreciates the opportunity to comment on your draft report.

Sincerely,

Jose D. Riojas
Chief of Staff

Enclosure

Enclosure

Department of Veterans Affairs (VA) Response to
Government Accountability Office (GAO) Draft Report
*MILITARY SEXUAL TRAUMA: Improvements Made, but VA Can Do More to Track
and Improve the Consistency of Disability Claim Decisions*
(GAO-14-477)

GAO Recommendation: **The Secretary of Veterans Affairs should direct the
Under Secretary for Benefits to:**

Recommendation 1: **expand existing training and guidance to adjudicators
responsible for MST-related claims by, for example, providing mandatory
refresher courses or regularly distributing examples of relevant errors identified
from quality assurance reviews.**

VA Comment: Concur. The Veterans Benefits Administration (VBA) is in the process
of creating an eLearning product for Military Sexual Trauma (MST) refresher training for
MST-related claims. The course will consist of four separate eLearning lessons, which
may be assigned individually or as a group. VBA expects to have the following lessons
completely developed and available to field personnel by August 15, 2014:

Course Title: Posttraumatic Stress Disorder Due to Military Sexual Trauma.

- Lesson 1: Introduction: Target audience is Claims Assistants, Veterans Service
  Representatives (VSR) and Rating Veterans Service Representatives (RVSR).
  Course duration is 20 minutes.
- Lesson 2: Rules and Regulations: Target audience is VSRs and RVSRs.
  Course duration is 30 minutes.
- Lesson 3: Development: Target audience is VSRs and RVSRs. Course
  duration is 40 minutes.
- Lesson 4: Rating: Target audience is RVSRs. Course duration undetermined.

Recommendation 2: **develop a plan for conducting more comprehensive quality
reviews of MST-related claims that allows the agency to identify problem areas,
target improvement efforts, and track performance over time.**

VA Comment: Concur. MST claims continue to be part of each regional office's
monthly quality sample. In addition, VBA has established and implemented a plan for
the Systematic Technical Accuracy Review (STAR) staff to conduct special focused
reviews for MST claims twice each year. These recurring, focused reviews will help
identify problem areas, target improvement efforts, and track performance over time.
The first review began in May 2014 and will focus on the root cause of why MST claims
are denied, as well as to assess whether the claims have been denied in error. The
second review will be conducted in the first quarter of fiscal year 2015 to analyze
regional office grant rates that are outside of the national statistical norm to determine
whether these types of claims receive an accurate decision. Within 4 months of
completion of each review, results will be updated in the systematic analysis identified in
Recommendation 4. VBA considers this recommendation fully implemented.

1

Department of Veterans Affairs (VA) Response to
Government Accountability Office (GAO) Draft Report
*MILITARY SEXUAL TRAUMA: Improvements Made, but VA Can Do More to Track
and Improve the Consistency of Disability Claim Decisions*
(GAO-14-477)

Recommendation 3: further analyze existing data on MST-related claim decisions
by, for example, determining approval rates by regional office and veteran
gender.

VA Comment: Concur. VBA pulled data to compare many claims processing metrics
and outcome measures for MST-related cases and is in the early stages of review. The
data produced include a review of approval rates by regional office and Veteran gender.
Additionally, VBA will continue to conduct consistency studies of the claims processing
personnel responsible for MST-related cases based on the results of the STAR special
review and data analysis. As noted in the response to Recommendation 2, VBA will
continue to look for opportunities to enhance its quality review program to allow us to
monitor the quality of claims processing over time. VBA's first analysis will be complete
by October 2014, with follow-up analyses every 6 months thereafter. Target Completion
Date: October 31, 2014.

Recommendation 4: explore ways to systematically collect additional data on
MST-related claims that might allow the agency to better track consistency. Such
data could include reasons for denials, whether claim evaluations included a
medical exam, and how often related medical exam reports are returned to VHA
for clarification or deemed insufficient.

VA Comment: Concur. VBA agrees with GAO that variations in the approval rates do
not necessarily mean that decisions were inaccurate. In conjunction with GAO's review,
VBA began to explore new ways to systematically collect additional data on MST-
related claims to promote improved consistency. VBA has commenced analyses of
claims processing metrics and outcomes for MST-related claims in order to compare
data. VBA looks for methods to identify whether MST claim denials were based on the
results of a medical examination or based on the claims processor's determination that
there was insufficient evidence to support an examination request, among other factors.

Working with the Veterans Health Administration (VHA), VBA will use the data from
these analyses to identify areas where variations in approval rates may result from
different interpretations of identifying markers, when to order exams, or how examiners
conduct the exams. The data will assist in the identification and implementation of
additional training to improve the development and rating processes for MST-related
claims. VBA's first analysis will be complete by October 2014, with follow-up analyses
every 6 months thereafter. Target Completion Date: October 31, 2014.

2

Department of Veterans Affairs (VA) Response to
Government Accountability Office (GAO) Draft Report
*MILITARY SEXUAL TRAUMA: Improvements Made, but VA Can Do More to Track
and Improve the Consistency of Disability Claim Decisions*
(GAO-14-477)

Recommendation 5: expand outreach to veterans who are eligible to resubmit
their previously denied PTSD claims related to MST. The agency should conduct
this outreach in partnership with the Veteran Health Administration or external
organizations, such as Veterans Service Organizations.

VA Comment: Concur. VBA has completed proactive outreach to Veterans who were
eligible to resubmit their previously denied posttraumatic stress disorder (PTSD) claims
related to MST. Over 2,600 letters were mailed to those Veterans who had previously
been denied claims related to MST. VBA is attempting to expand outreach to the
population of previously denied PTSD claims related to MST who filed prior to 2010. In
addition, VBA will continue to work closely with VHA, Veterans Service Organizations,
and other external partners to ensure this information is disseminated to Veterans so
that they may submit or resubmit a claim for PTSD related to MST. Target Completion
Date: September 30, 2014.

Recommendation 6: The Secretary for Veterans Affairs should further direct the
Under Secretary for Health to ensure that planned training on conducting
MST-related exams is provided to all medical examiners who perform them,
including contractors.

VA Comment: Concur. VHA is in the process of developing a training course focused
on training examiners to conduct trauma sensitive examinations for disability claims that
are filed secondary to an individual having experienced MST. The training course has
been approved and funded by the Office of Disability and Medical Assessment (DMA)
and the Employee Education System (EES).

The course will have a specific focus on training examiners who are conducting
Separation Health Examinations as individuals transition from active duty to Veteran
status.

The training course will be available to contracted examiners through VHA EES online
Talent Management System. The course will be electronically distributed to the four
contract vendors associated with DMA's Disability Exam Management Contract:

1. Quality. Timeliness. Customer Service.
2. Logistics Health Incorporated.
3. Veterans Evaluation Services.
4. Medical Support Los Angeles.

Target Completion Date: January 1, 2015.

3

Enclosure

Department of Veterans Affairs (VA) Response to
Government Accountability Office (GAO) Draft Report
*MILITARY SEXUAL TRAUMA: Improvements Made, but VA Can Do More to Track
and Improve the Consistency of Disability Claim Decisions*
(GAO-14-477)

Training will be completed by all medical examiners that perform MST-related exams.

Each Veterans Integrated Service Network (VISN) or vendor will be required to certify
that those examiners within their VISN or under a specific contract, who conduct
MST-related disability exams, have completed the training course. Target Completion
Date: April 30, 2015.

4

Appendix IV: GAO Contact and Staff Acknowledgments

GAO Contact	Daniel Bertoni, (202) 512-7215, or bertonid@gao.gov
Staff Acknowledgments	In addition to the contact named above, Michele Grgich (Assistant Director), Carl Barden, James Bennett, Susan Bernstein, Bianca Capone, William Colvin, Helen Desaulniers, Joel Green, Jonathan McMurray, Jean McSween, Nhi Nguyen, Almeta Spencer, Barbara Steel-Lowney, Walter Vance, Kathleen Van Gelder, and Craig Winslow made contributions to this report.

GAO's Mission	The Government Accountability Office, the audit, evaluation, and investigative arm of Congress, exists to support Congress in meeting its constitutional responsibilities and to help improve the performance and accountability of the federal government for the American people. GAO examines the use of public funds; evaluates federal programs and policies; and provides analyses, recommendations, and other assistance to help Congress make informed oversight, policy, and funding decisions. GAO's commitment to good government is reflected in its core values of accountability, integrity, and reliability.
Obtaining Copies of GAO Reports and Testimony	The fastest and easiest way to obtain copies of GAO documents at no cost is through GAO's website (http://www.gao.gov). Each weekday afternoon, GAO posts on its website newly released reports, testimony, and correspondence. To have GAO e-mail you a list of newly posted products, go to http://www.gao.gov and select "E-mail Updates."
Order by Phone	The price of each GAO publication reflects GAO's actual cost of production and distribution and depends on the number of pages in the publication and whether the publication is printed in color or black and white. Pricing and ordering information is posted on GAO's website, http://www.gao.gov/ordering.htm. Place orders by calling (202) 512-6000, toll free (866) 801-7077, or TDD (202) 512-2537. Orders may be paid for using American Express, Discover Card, MasterCard, Visa, check, or money order. Call for additional information.
Connect with GAO	Connect with GAO on Facebook, Flickr, Twitter, and YouTube. Subscribe to our RSS Feeds or E-mail Updates. Listen to our Podcasts. Visit GAO on the web at www.gao.gov.
To Report Fraud, Waste, and Abuse in Federal Programs	Contact: Website: http://www.gao.gov/fraudnet/fraudnet.htm E-mail: fraudnet@gao.gov Automated answering system: (800) 424-5454 or (202) 512-7470
Congressional Relations	Katherine Siggerud, Managing Director, siggerudk@gao.gov, (202) 512-4400, U.S. Government Accountability Office, 441 G Street NW, Room 7125, Washington, DC 20548
Public Affairs	Chuck Young, Managing Director, youngc1@gao.gov, (202) 512-4800 U.S. Government Accountability Office, 441 G Street NW, Room 7149 Washington, DC 20548